Backstreet Brother: ★ Aaron Carter

Corey Barnes

D1519999

Random House ⌂ New York

I wish to thank several important people without whose guidance, love, and support this book would not be possible: My parents, who have been in my corner every single day of my life, and my grandparents, who have always been more like parents than grandparents for as long as I can remember. To my other close family members and friends who have believed in me and encouraged me along the way: you've all stood by me for years and will always hold a special place in my heart. To my editor, Lisa, and her assistant, Kenneth, thank you for allowing me, like Aaron Carter, to turn a dream into reality.

Photograph credits: Front cover-top right: London Features International, Ltd./Sam Hain—LFI-UGS. Front cover-main: London Features International, Ltd./Anthony Cutajar. Back cover-top right: Star File Photo Agency/Jeffrey Mayer 1998. Page 1: London Features International, Ltd./NGI-London Features. Page 1: London Features International, Ltd./Anthony Cutajar—UCUT/LFI. Page 2: Star File Photo Agency/Guy Wade. Page 2: Star File Photo Agency/Guy Wade. Page 3: London Features International, Ltd./Anthony Cutajar—UCUT-LFI. Page 3: Star File Photo Agency/Jeffrey Mayer. Page 4: London Features International, Ltd./David Fischer—LFIDF. Page 4: London Features International, Ltd./Anthony Cutajar—UCUT-LFI. Page 5: London Features International, Ltd./Anthony Cutajar—UCUT. Page 6: London Features International, Ltd./NGI—London Features. Page 7 top-right: Star File Photo Agency/Jeffrey Mayer 1998. Page 7 main: London Features International, Ltd./Larry Marano—ULM/LFI. Page 7, bottom left: London Features International, Ltd./Sam Hain—LFI-UGS. Page 8: London Features International, Ltd./Ilpo Musto.

www.randomhouse.com/kids

ISBN: 0-375-80193-6
Library of Congress Catalog Card Number: 98-68131

Printed in the United States of America
10 9 8 7 6 5 4 3 2 1

Contents

1

Introducing: Aaron Carter!

"Attention! Attention! There is an intruder in the house!" calls a booming voice through the darkened concert hall. Everyone looks around as bright spotlights land on the audience. "What's this about an intruder?" fans are thinking. After all, this is a sold-out concert on the Backstreet Boys' very first full-length North American tour!

The gorgeous faces of the Backstreet Boys, the fabulous five otherwise known as Brian "B-Rok" Littrell, Howie "Sweet D" Dorough, A. J. "Bone" McLean, Nick "Chaos" Carter, and Kevin "The Train" Richardson, have been plastered on the covers of dozens of magazines from *Tiger Beat* to *Entertainment Weekly*. They've sold over 22 million records. Radio stations can't play enough of their hits. Their videos are constantly requested on MTV's *Total Request Live* countdown. Their home video, *All Access,* made it to the Top 10 list for home video purchases. In Canada, the Boys were even featured on Kellogg's Corn Pops cereal boxes. Usually, that honor is reserved for Olympic medalists, not pop groups. But this group is different!

For some fans in the audience, this was their first opportunity to catch a glimpse of their favorite group. Many of them had waited on line for hours to score tickets. Some fans even paid two hundred dollars for tickets from ticket brokers! *So what's this about an intruder?*

Suddenly, a pint-sized, blond-haired mini-babe bursts on stage, tearing through a white paper banner covered with colorful graffiti. *Who is he? Where'd he come from? How could such a young kid turn up as the opening act for such a world-famous group like the Backstreet Boys?*

Well, here's how: his name is Aaron Carter and he's the adorable younger brother of nineteen-year-old Nick, lead singer of the Backstreet Boys. Only eleven years old, he's already conquered the world, stealing the hearts of girls from Toledo to Tokyo. While most boys his age are riding their bikes, playing basketball, and hitting home runs, Aaron has been hitting the Top 10 charts in a serious way. Before he even turned ten, Aaron had a hit single on the Top 10 charts in Germany, Australia, the U.K., Norway, and Denmark! And, in addition to making hot dance records, Aaron himself has become a record—a record-breaker, that is! He won a place in the British edition of the *Guinness Book of World Records* for

being the youngest performer to have the most con-
secutive smash hits. He was even given a specially
engraved award to commemorate this feat.

But that's not all! Aaron had only been in the
music biz for a few months when he received several
other prestigious awards, including Golden Ottos
from *BRAVO* magazine in Germany and Spain. In
fact, he beat out his idol, singer Michael Jackson, as
well as actor/singer Will Smith! To top things off, the
German teen magazines *Popcorn* and *Pop/Rocky*
awarded Aaron the title of Best Singer, and RSH, a
German radio station, presented him with a gold tro-
phy!

"I always wanted to be just like Nick. He seemed
to have such a good time, and it looked like so much
fun," Aaron has said. "One time [Nick] left for a
whole year. He looked real different when he came
back and I said, 'You're not my brother!' He had to
show me an old picture before I believed him!"

One of the reasons Aaron probably wanted to be a
musician was to be closer to his beloved big brother.
Well, by the summer of 1998, Aaron was as close to
Nick as ever—opening for him on tour! Now Aaron
could shine in the spotlight, too!

The story you're about to read is about a little guy
who truly followed his heart and turned a dream into
a huge reality...

2
The Very Beginning

Aaron Charles Carter was born exactly two minutes after his fraternal twin sister, Angel, at Tampa General Children's Hospital on December 7, 1987. His parents, Robert (Bob) and Jane Carter, may have chosen the name "Aaron" because it's Mr. Carter's father's name. But the really cool thing about Aaron's name is that if you look it up in any American baby name book, you'll find it's actually a Biblical name that means *inspired*. The Carters sure did pick a fitting first name for their pop-star son! Also, Aaron's middle name is Charles, and according to American baby books, that means *strong*. Well, Aaron certainly is *strong* in the charts!

Aaron and Angel were the first Carter children to be born in a Florida hospital. Nick was born on January 28, 1980, in a Jamestown, New York, hospital (the same hospital as legendary Lucille Ball of *I*

Love Lucy!). Bobbie (also known as B. J.), who arrived two years later, was also born while the family still lived in Jamestown. As for middle sister Leslie, she was actually born at the Garden Villa Retirement Home in Florida, where Aaron's family worked and lived (more on that later!).

Since Nick was just a month away from his eighth birthday when the twins were born, he was old enough to remember some of the feelings he had when they arrived. It was a very special time for Nick. He had already experienced two other new additions to his family and survived losing his "only child" status as soon as B. J. and Leslie came into the world. He's often admitted that sharing the limelight was difficult at first, but soon he realized it was cool to have two younger sisters to play with.

However, when Aaron and Angel came along, it was a super shock to all three of the older Carter kids. They now had *twins* to contend with! But once they saw those two cute little bundles come home from the hospital, they probably figured, "The more the merrier!" Who could resist those little button noses and sweet coos? "When the twins came, that really affected everybody...I was excited to have another brother...I guess you could say it was a happy change," Nick has said.

Plenty of happy times lay ahead for the Carter family. They took fun trips to Universal Studios, went on boating excursions, camped out under the stars, and did loads of other fun-filled family activities.

Before Aaron and Angel arrived, the family had moved all the way south from their quiet country home in upstate New York. With their belongings packed into a trailer attached to the family's Cadillac Eldorado, the Carters drove over a thousand miles in search of a warmer climate and streets lined with palm trees. Their destination was sunny Florida, where Mr. Carter would begin a whole new career and his two sons' dreams of singing in front of huge audiences and selling thousands of records would become a reality. If a fortune-teller had revealed what was ahead for the Carter crew back then, they probably never would have believed it!

The family's first Florida residence was actually a home for senior citizens called the Garden Villa Retirement Home. They lived there for about a year. Aaron's mom, Jane, was the resident cook and his dad, Bob, was a manager. Jane must have been a great chef because Nick often tells reporters, "My mom's a really good cook!" She probably whipped up delicious and yummy meals that the elderly residents could look forward to. These days, Jane tries her best to make sure that Nick and Aaron's tour buses are equipped with a kitchen so she can cook them wholesome meals. It's very important for these growing guys to eat healthy foods, in order to keep up their strength! They also need a balanced diet to keep them from getting sick while traveling. It's not uncommon for groups who are touring to live on an unhealthy fast-food diet.

The retirement home was only big enough for about sixteen people, but this wasn't a problem for Mr. Carter. He simply extended the house so that everyone could live comfortably. Nick once said that his experiences as a young boy growing up around senior citizens taught him to be respectful and polite. Most kids aren't given such a great opportunity to be around older folks. Nick must have enjoyed being surrounded by different people from all walks of life. In turn, the elderly residents were probably anxious to share stories with him. There's no doubt they also appreciated his energetic, youthful ways.

After a year, the Carter family decided to move into their own home, but they still remained near the senior citizen residence. As Nick began to become famous, however, Mr. and Mrs. Carter knew they would have to devote most of their time to his career. Soon they made yet another important decision: they sold the retirement home. In the long run, they figured, it would be the best choice for the whole family, allowing them time to travel with Nick and care for little Aaron and his sisters. These days, if Bob or Jane has to be on the road with their sons, the kids' grandma comes down from New York to stay with the girls and make sure everything at home runs smoothly.

The family continued to live in the Tampa Bay area, which is located on the western coast of Florida in Hillsborough County. Thousands of curious tourists come to Tampa because there are so many cool places for people of all ages to visit. One of them is an amusement park called Busch Gardens. With tons of fantastic rides and safari excitement, Busch Gardens hosts some of the world's wildest roller coasters, like Montu and Kumba! Tampa is a very old city with an interesting history. One journalist decided to nickname Tampa "The Big Guava," a takeoff on New York City's title, "The Big Apple." In celebration of this, a Latin-style parade is held every year around Halloween in the downtown Tampa area of Ybor City. Another cool attraction is called the Gasparilla Pirate Fest. This event is held in Tampa once a year and draws nearly 400,000 people!

The palm tree–lined city attracts people from all over the world because of its beautiful beaches, historical museums, shops, piers, and boat marinas. Aaron says he especially likes spending time at one area hot spot called Shell Point Marina. He sometimes goes there with his family just to kick back for a day. It's a great place to unwind after a tour or studio session! At the marina, people can rent Jet Skis or just hang out, taking in some rays or dining at the marina's restaurant. Aaron used to do karaoke there. During one press conference, he mentioned singing a song by one of his faves, Tom Petty and the Heartbreakers.

Aaron's family spends most of their free time participating in nautical activities. His dad was once a scuba instructor and used to work on boats. Nick is also a certified scuba diver. Aaron really loves the ocean. So much, in fact, that he wouldn't mind studying the ocean and its brilliant sea life! In several interviews, Aaron has said that when he grows up, he might like to be a marine biologist.

Of course, Aaron has plenty of time to decide on a future career!

Since Aaron lives in a state where winter temperatures only reach a low of about 62 degrees, he sometimes must wonder what it'd be like to see snow outside his window. Believe it or not, there was a time at the beginning of his career when he had never even seen snow! He told a *Live & Kicking* reporter that he was very disappointed when he visited Austria and did not see any of the pretty white stuff. If the Carter family had remained living at their first address on Webber Road in Jamestown, Aaron could have enjoyed plenty of snowy upstate New York winters!

Aaron has to enjoy touring to snowy areas like Vermont and Canada, where he can snowboard, ski, and make snowmen. Snowy weather isn't always fun and games, though. When Aaron was filming a music video in Vancouver, Canada, he got stuck in the snow!

It was in Jamestown that Bob Carter and the kids' grandpa owned a small restaurant lounge called the Yankee Rebel. When big brother Nick was only two, he loved to spend time there. He has frequently talked about dancing up a storm on the Yankee Rebel's tiny dance floor! "We had a little dance floor at the Yankee Rebel and my dad used to be a DJ and play records. When I was real small, I used to get up there in my diapers and dance around," he told *SuperTeen*. It was there that Nick also discovered Pac-Man. "There I was in my white diaper, sitting on a stool playing a game. That is where my love for video games began!" Nick joked—and it seems he's passed that same passion on to Aaron!

For the past five years, when Aaron and his big bro aren't globetrotting, they have lived with the rest of the family in a lovely wooden house that's next to an inlet of water in a very quaint, quiet community called Ruskin. The brothers share a bedroom. Aaron told *YTV* that it's actually like a double-decker room with a loft that gives each of the guys a bit of privacy. Their room is painted green. Aaron has taped up several Spice Girls posters on the wall, and the guys' CDs and video games are stacked high in various areas of the room. Aaron usually keeps his sax and guitar in this room.

When a reporter from *Top of the Pops* magazine asked Aaron to describe what it's like sharing a room with his older bro, he replied, "It's cool. I wouldn't want a room on my own. I think I'd be bored...he's not going to [move out], he told me! He wouldn't want such a big room to himself, anyway. He's quite untidy, though, and sometimes it makes me mad—but not *really* mad."

Aaron's bedroom is also a refuge of a different sort. Aaron once confessed in *Top of the Pops* magazine that the spot under his bed had special importance: "(That's) where I hide when I don't want Mom to catch me…in case I've been naughty!" Since the humidity in Florida can make for sticky weather, Aaron loves the fact that his room is equipped with a large air conditioner: "I love it in there!" he said in the same article. "It's nice and cold because of the air conditioning!"

When Nick turned seventeen, he bought his family an eighteen-foot boat. It's docked next to a Jet Ski and other smaller boats in back of the Carters' house. Often parked in the spacious driveway are Mrs. Carter's white car, Nick's forest green truck, and a black Corvette. Aaron told *Live & Kicking* magazine: "Nick was gonna get a blue one, but they didn't have any left." He went on to say that when Nick is home, he sometimes takes Aaron for rides in his cool sports car!

As for the Carters' house, the boys' mother has said that, in the last couple of years, their home in Ruskin has truly become a Florida landmark! Back in April 1998, she said in a Yahoo!/ParentTime chat: "It has become a tourist attraction. The day Nick was to arrive home [from a tour], we had a hundred people outside with banners welcoming him. Before that, there were fifty people a day. We always keep autograph cards there and we give them out. If he's there, he sometimes goes out to say 'hi' to them. [Fans] usually know they can catch him if he's at home. When he walks down the driveway to get the mail, there's always somebody with a video camera taping him."

Surrounding Aaron's home is a very high security

fence, complete with a special entry gate to keep curious fans from roaming the grounds. *Teen Machine* magazine has reported that fans have been known to pull grass and flowers from the Carters' lawn. Once, someone actually stole Nick's basketball! An area gas station owner has told journalists that young girls from all over the world constantly stop in and ask him where they can find Aaron's house. There have also been reports of people charging for bus tours to the Carters' home!

In an interview with radio station KTU, the Backstreet Boys revealed that at one of their shows a fan was holding a sign with a large photo of Nick's house glued to it. The caption next to the photo read "I was there!" One can only imagine the look on Nick's face when he turned to Brian and said, "My house is in the audience!"

Despite all of this, there have been rumors that Aaron and his family may actually be moving to Los Angeles in the near future—Aaron may star in his very own sitcom!

The Carter brothers try their best not to turn fans away. But their mom sometimes politely asks fans to leave them alone when they're dining in public. A quiet family meal should be kept private.

Living such a public life must be difficult, but the brothers know that without their fans they wouldn't be as popular as they are today. So they do try to give back as much as they possibly can. Their mom agrees that fans are very important to her sons. During the

Yahoo!/ParentTime online chat, she said, "Without the fans, they're nothing. If you're not good to your fans, you don't need to be in the business. You have to show them appreciation of everything they give you."

3
Big Bro Paves the Road to Success

The Carters have always been a musical family. In an interview with a Canadian music television program, Nick pointed out that both his mother and father had been involved in the business. Jane was involved in drama when she was younger and, much like Nick, Bob was in a rock 'n' roll band in his teens. But the performing roots go back even further. Years ago, Nick and Aaron's maternal grandfather received a master's degree in drama, in both acting and directing plays. Even the boys' maternal great-grandfather, Robert Neal, was involved in music. He played the organ and sang in the church choir for over twenty years.

With all this musical talent in his blood *and* an older brother who happened to be an adored member of the Backstreet Boys, there was no way Aaron could help but want to follow in his big brother's footsteps.

In an interview with *Top of the Pops* magazine, Aaron confessed, "If Nick wasn't a singer, then I wouldn't be here. He supports me and is the one who asked me if I wanted to sing. I was interested in performing before, but I think it would have been a lot harder."

Nick has been active in the entertainment industry for as long as Aaron can remember. Aaron can probably recall plenty of times when someone would turn on the TV and, lo and behold, there would be Nick's familiar face smiling away! In his early years, Nick starred in commercials, too, including TV ads for a local lottery and the Money Store. Aaron may even have been sitting on his mom's lap in the football stands, cheering not just for the family's favorite team, but also for Nick, who was part of the vocal entertainment during the Tampa Bay Buccaneers halftime show!

Nick officially signed with the Backstreet Boys when Aaron was about four years old. Growing up around all that excitement *had* to have been an inspiration for Aaron to sing. If Nick could do it, so could Aaron!

At the tender age of five, while he was just a kindergarten student at Frank D. Miles Elementary School, Aaron told his parents how much he wanted to get involved in singing. He hadn't had many lessons, but deep down he knew that this was what he wanted to do.

Many parents wouldn't have been as understanding as Mrs. Carter. She must have seen a sparkle in Aaron's eye—the same one that had flickered in Nick's when he was a youngster. In an interview with *YT*, Aaron recalled the chain of events: "When I decided I wanted to be a singer...my mom encouraged me to start a band. By the time I was seven, I was the lead singer of a group called Dead End! It was great fun!"

Aaron attended a rock music school near his home called Yamaha's Rock School at Paragon, which is where he met the three other guys who made up Dead End. The group used to entertain at local libraries and cafés. Dead End once performed at the Rock School for about two hundred people. Aaron remembers that particular performance as his first time in front of a large audience. Little did he know then that, in just a very short time, he'd be singing and dancing for foreign audiences of fifty thousand people!

Dead End reached a real dead end after about two years. The group split up because of their musical differences, which was not surprising. Young musicians are just beginning to figure out what type of music best defines them. Aaron, being the lead singer of Dead End, must have felt that he wasn't following the creative route he really wanted to take. He wanted to follow a more urban/dance/techno route, while the other members preferred alternative rock, such as Nirvana and Green Day. Aaron described his decision in *Top of the Pops*: "I left, as they wanted to do alternative music and I wanted to do more pop."

Often, members of a group decide to go solo and, in the long run, find there's less tension and more fun in being independent. Aaron must have known that, even though he wasn't a member of a rock group, he'd still make it in the music biz. Going solo was an important step for Aaron, and he was ready for it. His dedication and determination would help him achieve success—on his own!

Though he seemed born with a natural ability to sing and dance like a pro, Aaron realized the importance of formal training, thanks to his brother Nick. Nick's fabulous voice was improved through lessons from a vocal coach, June Daniels, whom his mom had found in the yellow pages. Ms. Daniels played the piano for Nick while he sang songs from *Mary Poppins,* such as "Feed the Birds" (his mom still has his old sheet music!).

At first, June thought Nick was a bit too young for serious training, but after a few lessons she quickly saw that he had incredible potential. Nick's next vocal coach, Mary-Ann, also helped him perfect his craft. Following Nick's example, Aaron learned that only a trained professional could teach him scales and the proper means of harmonizing. "Vocal lessons were what I really needed. I can hit the notes now. The trouble I used to have was breathing, but now I can do it better," he reported in an interview in *16* magazine.

After plenty of hard work, Aaron's big break finally happened. In March 1997, during a special appearance at the Backstreet Boys' concert in Berlin, Germany, Aaron literally stumbled into the big time, singing and dancing his heart out, even though he was merely nine years old. Not one person in the audience could sit still. His darling voice and angelic face drove the fans—especially the females—wild! That night's performance was filled with cool, funky cartwheels and sizzling, danceable beats. It was no wonder that Aaron single-handedly stole the show *and* the hearts of probably every girl in the audience—not to mention the undivided attention of a very important person who would soon turn young Aaron's fantasy of being a star into a reality.

As fate would have it, an executive from the Edel Record Company in Germany, an ultra-hip record label whose other young clients included the adorable boy band Take 5 and Top 10 recording artist Jennifer Paige, was in the house. The executive offered Aaron a record deal right there after the show!

With his first record deal, Aaron knew it was time to get a manager. That's when Johnny Wright of Wright Stuff Management, who then managed both the Backstreet Boys and 'N Sync, and Mom stepped in. Big brother Nick also lent a hand in supervising Aaron's career. Aaron considers him to be a major player in his management team. Now that Johnny Wright is no longer managing Aaron, it has become a family affair!

With Aaron's vocal training well under way, it was time to think about his dance moves. Much of the fancy footwork he does onstage and in videos is either self-taught or passed on from his choreographer. Like other performers, Aaron has someone to help him with the more complicated routines. That way, he knows which dance steps work better with each song. He's also prone to throwing in those one-handed cartwheels and handstands!

During the fall of 1997, Aaron released his first single, "Crush on You," overseas. The song was originally a big hit for an eighties group called the Jets and soon proved to be a huge success again for the nine-year-old Aaron. The next release was the bouncy, upbeat tune "Crazy Little Party Girl." Both songs became instant favorites and won Aaron fans from all over the globe. The two hits sizzled on the foreign Top 10 charts in countries like Germany, Australia, the U.K., Norway, and Denmark. Aaron's third single, "I'm Gonna Miss You Forever," was his first soft love song, which soon climbed the German charts. Another single, "Shake It," which features the Miami group 95 South, also became very popular. Almost all of Aaron's very successful videos were directed by Lionel Martin, who also directed videos for the Backstreet Boys.

Aaron's debut album, appropriately named "Aaron Carter," also included the easy-to-dance-to "Swing It Out" and a remake of the New Kids on the Block hit "Please Don't Go, Girl." There is one particular song on Aaron's CD that must be very special to him. It's called "Ain't That Cute" and it was written by Nick and best bud Brian Littrell. Nick, Brian, and the other Backstreet Boys are at the top of Aaron's thank-you list on the inside pamphlet that comes with his album. This pamphlet also features adorable pictures of Aaron on the beach and with Pepper, his mini schnauzer. The album was produced by Gary Carolla, who has also done work with 'N Sync and other Trans Continental Records' groups. Mr. Carolla took Aaron under his wing, and the two must have had a blast working together. Aaron thanked Gary on his album liner notes, saying that Gary had even taught him his jokes! Fans abroad were lucky to get in on Aaron's musical mastering a whole lot earlier than U.S. fans did. Aaron's album didn't hit U.S. stores until June 16, 1998. The CD went gold in Spain, Norway, Canada, Denmark, and Germany.

Aaron performed a variety of his hits during his summer tour in 1998. "Surfin' USA," the remake of a classic sixties Beach Boys tune, was released as a single after his album came out. Aaron sometimes surprised fans by including it in his 1998 tour routine.

Because he was such an instant sensation all over Europe, Aaron was selected to work on a very special project with the Backstreet Boys, 'N Sync, the Moffatts, and several other foreign pop stars such as Gil and Scooter. Together they went by the name Bravo All Stars and recorded a beautiful song called "Let the Music Heal Your Soul" that became a Top 10 hit in Germany, Norway, Spain, and Switzerland. It was later released in the U.S. on November 3, 1998. All of the groups donated their time and fantastic voices to benefit the Nordoff-Robbins Music Therapy

Foundation. This foundation helps disabled and autistic children through the use of a specially developed form of music therapy. Nordoff-Robbins fund-raising events have been strongly supported by other famous musicians, including Aerosmith and Bon Jovi. It must have been a great experience for Aaron to work with his brother Nick, as well as other hot young recording artists from all over the world!

Aaron has a lot of big plans in the works for the future. Right now there's talk of a duet with Nick, a second album, as well as rumors of a television show and even a possible movie about the Carter boys. Only time will tell what's next for this rising superstar. Aaron's already proved he's willing to work hard and eager to try new things, so the sky's the limit!

4

Aaron Answers Your Personal Questions

Can you imagine actually meeting Aaron in person? After the initial shock wore off, you'd probably want to ask him a million different questions. He's achieved so much for someone who's only eleven: What's it like being so famous at such a young age? What does he like best about touring? What's it like having Nick as a big brother? Your list of questions could go on and on to the point that you'd probably end up being escorted away from the little cutie! Here are some questions you might want answered, based on actual interviews with Aaron. If you can think of some that aren't mentioned, you might want to race ahead to Chapter 12 and write Aaron a letter. That way you can ask him the questions that are most important to *you!*

★ *Aaron Dishes on His Sibs!* ★

Does Nick ever do anything that makes you mad?

Naturally, all brothers love to go after each other—even famous brothers! *"He locks me out of the house!"* Aaron confessed in a *Live & Kicking* interview. *"When we play hide-and-seek he'll say, 'I'm it!' and then run off, leaving me hiding. I'll be sitting there all cramped up for two or three hours and he'll never come and find me!"* Aaron once told a Canadian music television reporter, *"He throws me in the pool all the time! Even if it's freezing cold!"* Purely a case of "boys will be boys."

But Aaron reports to *Live & Kicking* that he does his share of pestering Nick, too, and has even been known to push his big brother into the water!

Can you give some examples as to how Nick is messier than you are?

"When he comes home, he trashes [the room]! He puts out his suitcase, pulls out the clothes, throws them every-where...and he never makes the bed, which makes Mom go, 'Ahhh!'" (YTV)

When you were younger, did your mom dress you and Angel alike?

"Yep," Aaron told *Live & Kicking. "But she had pink and I had blue."*

Who do you think is wackier, you or Nick?

"Nick!" Aaron replied with a laugh when a *TV Hits* journalist asked him this interesting question. *"But maybe I'll get as crazy as him when I'm older! Nick's crazy on paintballing…he was playing in a paintball war and got hit on his leg. He had four pairs of pants on, but it went through all his pants…and he got a real huge cut and bruise."*

Do your sisters ever feel left out because you and Nick are so famous?

"No, because everyone's doing their own thing," Aaron answered in an interview in *Top of the Pops* magazine. *"My twin sister, Angel, is going to try modeling, and my older sister Bobbie isn't really into music. Leslie, my other older sister, wants to sing and she might be doing backing vocals on my next single…"*

Do you and your twin sister Angel get along well?

"Yes, but she's the complete opposite of myself," Aaron told *TV Hits. "She's very calm…and as she was born two minutes before me, she always looks after me like a mother goose."*

Aside from Ninja Turtles, are there any other toys that you love?

"Me and Nick have started collecting Beanie Babies. Nick has around 80, but I've only got 10. There is one called Britannia Bear, which we both really want. I hope I get it first!" This question and answer appeared in the June 1998 issue of Aaron's official newsletter, and since then, the guys have collected tons more Beanie Babies!

Has Nick done anything to help further your career or given you any advice?

"Nick has helped me so much," Aaron told YT. "He's my business manager. He gives me great advice and keeps me on track with my career. If it wasn't for him, I wouldn't be so famous." He also told Big!, "I just hope to be as successful as Nick...he's really supportive and even appears in my video." When asked this same question by a TV Hits reporter, Aaron talked about one important piece of advice Nick has given him that he will never forget: "When I'm just about to go on stage, he'll come up and sit me down all serious and go, 'Now, don't worry, just imagine there's only two or three people out there and sing to them.' It really works—it stops me from getting too nervous. He's so good like that. I really couldn't ask for a better brother."

Will Nick have anything to do with your next album?

"*Nick did background vocals on my first album, and he's also one of my producers,*" Aaron revealed to a *SuperTeen* reporter. "*When you put Nick's voice over mine, we sound like the same person.*"

What's the difference between you and Nick?

"*He's older,*" Aaron quipped during an interview with *Teen Beat.* "*I'm more outgoing and he's shy.*"

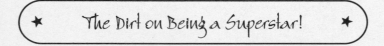

★   The Dirt on Being a Superstar!   ★

What is the best thing about being a star?

"*Being able to meet my fans, going around the world, and visiting countries. I think it's a good feeling because no other ten-year-old boy gets to perform onstage!*" Aaron told *superstars* magazine.

Describe an average day for you.

"*I do interviews…and TV shows and photo sessions,*" Aaron told *SuperTeen.* "*It's a lot of fun. But most reporters ask the same questions. They want to talk about Nick all the time, and they give me letters to give him.*"

Do you think you'll ever get sick of being famous?

"Probably not," Aaron told a *TV Hits* reporter. *"I love what I do, and I think I'll want to do it for a long time yet. I can't ever imagine getting bored."*

Sometimes rock stars like to trash their hotel rooms. What's the wildest thing you've ever done?

"I had the music up really loud when I was in a hotel room in Madrid once," Aaron confessed to *Top of the Pops.* *"The people next door called the desk and complained. I was listening to Metallica while jumping around on the bed, and when the guy came and knocked on the door, I hid...I lifted the TV out of the cabinet and crawled in there [to hide]!"*

Who are some of the famous people you've met since you've become a star?

"I've met Aqua, Robyn Hitchcock, Coolio, Jeff Goldblum, Ginuwine, and 'N Sync," Aaron told *SuperTeen.* *"['N Sync] came to my school party!"*

What do you spend your money on?

"I don't keep the money in my pockets," Aaron told British reporters. *"My mom and dad keep it...it's in the bank."*

Is it hard to learn a new song or remember the words to some of your songs?

"I can learn a song in five minutes, no problem," Aaron told a *YT* reporter. *"Also, if you show me a note on the guitar, I can copy it right away. Remembering things is easy."*

Is it hard to remember your routine when you get onstage?

"It is kind of hard trying to remember what you're going to do, like what song comes next. As for the words, I just memorize them," Aaron said in *Tiger Beat.*

Did you do anything special to celebrate having a Top 10 hit single?

"I went out to a restaurant with some of my friends and met some of the fans who had bought my records," Aaron told *Top of the Pops.* Unlike older musicians who throw huge bashes or spend the night out on the town, Aaron had a quiet evening. *"I usually have to be in bed by 10:00 P.M., but this time I stayed up all night. That was because I was leaving the hotel at five in the morning so there was no point sleeping. My mom's usually there to make sure I go to bed..."*

Would you say that Nick's fans are also fans of your music?

"Yeah," he admitted in an interview with *TV Hits.* *"I do seem to get a lot of his fans liking me, but there's also*

a lot who don't like Nick. That's pretty cool, isn't it?" Aaron joked.

Where are the coolest places you've visited?

"I've been to so many…England, France, Spain, Denmark…everywhere. It's been really good. I've been having lots of fun," Aaron told *SuperTeen.* *"I've been to Hawaii, even. But of all the places I really like Munich. It was snowing, but it wasn't that cold. I love snow. I love hearing different languages in Europe. It's strange, but I have managed to pick some up. I can speak a little German, Dutch, and Swedish now."*

★ Aaron Spills the Beans on the Backstreet Boys! ★

Do you have any funny stories about the Backstreet Boys?

In the March 1998 issue of *Big!* magazine, Aaron confessed, *"Nick and Brian always try to tickle me, and A. J. tells me to buy a hat every time I see him!"*

Who's the wackiest Backstreet Boy?

"A. J.!" Aaron told a foreign reporter. *"He's really crazy! He, like, walks around going, 'Mmmblllbrrb' [silly*

mumbling noise] and pulling all these weird kinds of faces. And he always wears sunglasses, even indoors! But he's really good fun, too!"

Are you close to the Boys? Do they treat you like a little brother?

"Oh, yeah," he told *SuperTeen*. "All the Backstreet Boys treat me like a little brother."

If you could be any of the Backstreet Boys, aside from Nick, who would it be?

That's a pretty cool question, don't you think? Aaron told *Live & Kicking* it'd have to be Brian! Why? *"Because he's got a good voice and my twin sister, Angel, thinks he's cute."* Awww!

How would you describe each of the Backstreet Boys?

"Nick is hyper-man. Howie is sweet. Kevin is serious. Brian is funny, and A. J. is crazy," Aaron said in *superstars* magazine.

5
The Carter Family Squeals on Aaron!
Here's What His Family Has to Say:

★ From Aaron's Mom and Dad: ★

What was Aaron like as a little boy?

"He was a little mischievous," Jane told *Tiger Beat.* *"He's a lot more outgoing than Nick and he gets into a lot more trouble than Nick did, but of course Nick got into his share of trouble, too."*

How would you describe Aaron?

"Aaron is very quick, with an imaginative mind, and he's smart…Aaron is a natural actor, comedian, and also a dramatic talent…He's more outgoing, maybe more than Nick, and he's also a bit more aggressive," Aaron's dad told Henrick Vartanian, a reporter for DIO.

Even though Nick and Aaron are famous, can they still maintain regular friendships?

Jane addressed this question in an online chat with Yahoo!/ParentTime back in April of 1998: *"Nick and Aaron have lots of friends. When Nick comes home, all the guys…come to the house and take him out to play basketball and hang around the house. Nick's always been really easy to get along with…Aaron makes a lot of friends out on the road. He's so outgoing!"*

How do Nick and Aaron get along?

"…Nick and Aaron are very close and love each other a lot. Nick worries about him and gives him advice," Bob told the DIO reporter. *"The age difference between them is not an issue. Nick still plays Ninja Turtles with Aaron,"* added Jane.

★   From Aaron's Twin Sis, Angel: ★

What's it like to be Aaron and Nick's sister?

"It's okay. But because I knew them before all this started, I don't think of them as being really, really famous. It was weird at first, but we've all gotten used to it now. We still fight and hit each other," Angel joked to a reporter. *"Nick's not at home much, but he still acts the same and*

Aaron's still a bit of a goofball...[My friends] think they're normal, just like I do!"

★ From Big Bro, Nick: ★

How would you *describe Aaron?*

"Basically he's a little blond...dancing and singing fool! That's what he is," Nick confessed in *SuperTeen.* *"I love him, he's my little brother."*

How do you advise him, since you have so much experience in the music business?

"The business can be very stressful and hard," Nick said on the Canadian music program *Musique Plus.* *"To make it as young as he did, he does have to have his schooling and my mom and dad there with him. I'm going to always be there for him and to support and to protect him from the bad things that can be in the business."*

In a press conference before the Backstreet Boys' 1998 summer tour, Nick had this to say on the subject of his little bro: *"I've gone through a lot of the same...And being that he wants to do the same thing, why not pass a little bit of what I know and lead him past all the rocky roads?...I wrote a song with Brian on Aaron's album and I'm already preparing* to write some more songs for his next album."

Do you see a lot of yourself in Aaron?

"I definitely see the urge of him wanting to do it…to be just as successful as I wanted to be back then," Nick told SuperTeen.

6

What's in the Stars for Aaron?

Aaron: Astrologically Speaking!

There are so many special meanings surrounding a person's birthday. Aside from your basic zodiac sign, some people believe that even the very day you were born can be associated with certain characteristics and personality traits. Aaron was born on December 7. According to numerologists, people born on the seventh day of the month can sometimes be perfectionists. This could be true for Aaron—he's not one to give something a less than 100 percent effort! He puts all of his energy into whatever he's doing and won't rest until it's perfect. When rehearsing for a concert, Aaron goes through his dance moves and practices over and over until each note and step are just right.

Another trait associated with people born on the seventh day of the month is the ability to reason well.

That may be why Aaron has often insisted that when it comes to school, math is his favorite subject. Everyone knows you need to be able to analyze complicated problems and follow difficult formulas in mathematics.

Another common trait among those born on this day is an ability to sense the future. Aaron often said early in his career that he wanted to be just like Nick and travel the world singing and dancing for fans. He must have had some vision that all his hard work would someday pay off. Astrologists also warn those born on the seventh to "follow hunches"—and that's exactly what Aaron did. Talk about being right on target!

Sensitivity is another personality trait associated with Aaron's birth date. Those who have met Aaron know he's got a vulnerable side. He doesn't like it if his brother kids him too much when they play. And like most people, Aaron doesn't enjoy being picked on or being treated like a baby. Even though Aaron is the youngest of the Carter crew—and being the youngest usually means taking orders—numerologists say that 7's don't always take orders well. To make up for this, they may actually try to turn a situation into one where they have the upper hand!

Another characteristic 7's share is stubbornness. Aaron doesn't seem very headstrong. If he is, it's obviously worked to his advantage, making him pursue success until he achieved it! Aaron knew that he became a star at a younger age than almost any other pop music performer. In fact, because he was only nine when he first hit it big overseas, Aaron was two years younger than Zac of Hanson when Hanson began hitting the charts in 1997 with "MMMBop"! In the entertainment world, sometimes being stubborn can be a positive trait, even though people usually tend to think of it as a bad thing.

★　　　　**Aaron the Sagittarius guy!**　　　　★

Symbol: The Archer.

Element: Fire.

Gem: Turquoise.

Flower: Carnation.

Positive Personality Traits:
Honest, friendly, warm, chatty, smart, optimistic, generous, and kind.

Negative Personality Traits:
Rebellious, can have a tough time keeping secrets, stubborn, and blunt.

Aaron was born on December 7, 1987, which makes him a Sagittarius. Sagittarius is the ninth sign of the zodiac and the sign of philosophy and religion.

Astrologists believe that Sagittarians use wisdom to understand the world, since they're considered the scholars and learners of the zodiac. They're known to explore and look for meanings behind things. They also highly value schooling and learning.

The Archer, a figure that's half man and half horse, is used to symbolize Sagittarius. These beasts, also known as "centaurs," were the great intellectuals of Greek and Roman myth, but they could also be a bit wild. Many Sagittarians in general aren't considered to be prejudiced or overly opinionated. They also don't set their plans in stone, but prefer to accept new things as they appear, which seems to be true in Aaron's case. He has never taken any dance lessons! Instead, he uses his natural ability and learns as he goes along, with a little help from his choreographers.

Sagittarians love freedom. They don't exactly enjoy being bossed around or forced to do things. Aaron is the first to admit that he sometimes can be a bit too adventurous. Mrs. Carter has said that he can be aggressive and sometimes mischievous. "He can be a real handful," Mrs. Carter has said. "He *can* be good, but he can be real naughty...he's always running away from his bodyguard." When it's time to attempt a dangerous stunt, you can count on Aaron to be the fearless one! He's the first one to try a new dive in his pool or test out a funky new toy. Like most eleven-year-old boys, Aaron loves doing what he wants without having to listen to reason—such as running around without a bodyguard. This is a major quality of people who share the sign of Sagittarius.

Independence is something that describes Sagittarians to a T—and that's also Aaron! He loves to explore and do whatever he can without the help of someone older.

Even as a tot, Aaron loved to do his own thing. Being independent can lead to trouble, but independence is also a good thing. The little events in his life that may have caused Aaron to be punished or sent to his room without dessert are all learning experiences. Trying out new things on your own is something Sagittarians just feel the need to do.

Sagittarians can sometimes be a little bossy and impatient when it comes to getting what they want. All zodiac signs have something "not so nice" about them, so don't look at these statements as a dis on adorable little Aaron. It's just that, maybe if a Sag is not winning at basketball, he'll, um...adjust the rules a little or make friendly suggestions about how things should be done so that he'll win. Hey, that's only normal, right? Who wants to wait around or be bossed around?

Sags also tend to put things off until the last possible minute. Aaron himself has said that he doesn't exactly love doing homework, and there have been times when he has finished it all on time. But putting things off isn't always a sign of laziness. Aaron is far from being a slacker. He's just got so many things going on in his life!

Sagittarians *may* seem extravagant and flashy, but on the other hand, they're usually good-humored and generous. They are sometimes the first ones to offer their help to those in need. In Aaron's case, that meant participating in the Bravo All-Stars project to help less fortunate children. He's often made statements in interviews that depict his generous and giving nature. In July 1998, he said, "If I could change the world, I'd like to help people who are dying from AIDS and cancer. Sickness is what I'd like to change. Every [sickness] there is. If I ever made enough money, I'd give it to every single charity."

Sagittarius is ruled by the planet Jupiter. In ancient Roman mythology, Jupiter was the planet of luck, which can be easily linked to Aaron. He has talked about run-ins with sharks while out on the boat with his family, and surviving them scratch-free. He also suffered a near-death experience when he almost drowned in a pool. So luck has been on his side, big time!

The element associated with Sagittarius is fire. Fire signs are known to be physical, tending to respond to the world through action. Again, this is totally Aaron! He's full of energy, and reporters have talked freely in magazines about how getting the little guy to sit still for more than a minute is impossible!

People born under this sign want to experience life, rather than read about it. Aaron enjoys visiting different cities and meeting new people in foreign countries. His tutor has even set up his assignments around actual historical places he's visited so he can get enthusiastic about these lessons. She also has him keep a journal so he won't forget them, either.

Sagittarians are famous for being outgoing and friendly. Aaron has so many friends from all over the world. When he visits different cities to perform, he tries to make a point of hanging with those who are dear to him. He must really love taking part in Meet 'n Greets. Meet 'n Greets allow him to say "Waaass up" to his dedicated fans, as well as shake their hands, hug them, and of course either autograph a picture of himself or a copy of his CD for them.

Other things you should know about Sagittarians are that they're open-minded and enthusiastic, but they may sometimes seem to let their mouths get them into trouble. They tend to talk way too much or speak before thinking. When he's constantly grilled about big bro Nick, he might give away a secret or two. Whoops! In July 1998, Aaron said, "When Nick comes home, it's like a tornado's passed by." Then there's the time he talked to British reporters about his big sister Leslie's love life! "I know a secret," Aaron whispered. "She has a boyfriend and his name is Jason!" These obviously are innocent examples of the Sagittarius "foot in mouth" problem. Most likely, his

siblings weren't too upset with their little brother—
well, unless, of course, Leslie's man checks the foreign
teen mags!

Sagittarians are positive thinkers. They're simply
born optimistic and love to look on the bright side.
Anyone who's ever met Aaron or seen him in television interviews knows he's happy-go-lucky. While
filming his video "Crazy Little Party Girl" in
Vancouver, Canada, it was extremely cold and snowy.
In fact, Aaron even got stuck in the snow a couple of
times while trying to perform different moves the
video called for! However, he didn't let the cold and
snow get him down. Many performers would have
complained or refused to work in such conditions.
But not this Carter cutie, who was all smiles and just
seemed to effortlessly go with the flow. It's not every
day this Floridian gets to play in the snow!

One thing Sagittarians have to watch out for is
their habit of being a little too straightforward and
tactless. Once, Aaron told a foreign reporter that her
jacket was "out of style." Since he was only nine when
he made that statement, one can't help but laugh.
There was also a time in April 1998 when a British
reporter kept grilling him on why he preferred female
fans to male fans. This caused Aaron to blurt out, "It's
a natural habit—I don't know!" This was a rather silly
question, so who could blame him for getting a tad
angry?

Sagittarians love to make people laugh. Astrologists say they're natural comedians who tend to sometimes exaggerate situations to entertain people. Aaron seems to fit easily into that category. An article in *Live & Kicking* magazine, titled "Aaron's Tall Tales," starts off with the question "Have you ever broken anything and said 'Nope, it wasn't me!'?" To that, Aaron answered, "A lamp my grandpa made. I was playing basketball in the house with my twin sister, Angel, and I hit the ball real hard against the wall. It bounced off and *Bam!*...my mom never did find out. I told her it was our two big dogs that did it!" In the same article, Aaron also revealed that he once exaggerated to the press, "I caught a nine-foot shark with my bare hands, but I didn't really. It was only a nine-inch shark." In another interview, a reporter asked: "How often do you tell fibs?" Aaron had no problem "fessing up." He said, "Every day. Big fibs!...I said in a magazine that I'd been swimming with dolphins, because I wanted to sound cool, but then my mom read it and she was like, 'What?' I have swum with a manatee, though! They weigh about one ton...about a hundred million of me!" To that statement, the writer added the hilarious comment "Clearly fibbing again!"

Sagittarians are also born with a sense of inner confidence that shows when they communicate with others. They can often be flirtatious and enjoy socializing immensely. Aaron seems to love mingling with people and apparently loves tagging along with Nick. Nick's talked openly about Aaron doing cartwheels all over the place when he's around the Backstreet Boys. That's fine with them. They love Aaron and it shows. They agreed to let him open for them on their German Open Air tour, as well as on their first full-length North American tour!

Sagittarians love participating in sports. Aaron would probably never pass up the chance to go one-on-one with Nick on the basketball court. People born under this sign simple adore a personal challenge! The freaky thing about Aaron is, as you know, he absolutely loves fishing. He has even said his cast net is one of his prized possessions. Well, according to astrology, Sagittarians enjoy solitary sports that test their personal strengths, and fishing has been linked as a hobby of this birth sign. Talk about a coincidence! Isn't that just downright freaky?

A great strength of the Sagittarius-born is their deep exploratory nature. It's important to them that they experience everything they can. They have a great love of knowledge and imagination, which makes them one of the most intellectual characters of the zodiac. Aaron's a perfect candidate for that!

When it comes to his schoolwork, the littlest Carter doesn't have much of a problem. He's admitted to loving math and fractions and can learn music in record time. *SuperTeen* reporters asked him how long he rehearses his songs before going into the studio to record them. He answered, "Not at all! I get the song one day before recording if I'm lucky!" He's also said

On location
with Mom
and Dad.

Aaron gets
wild!

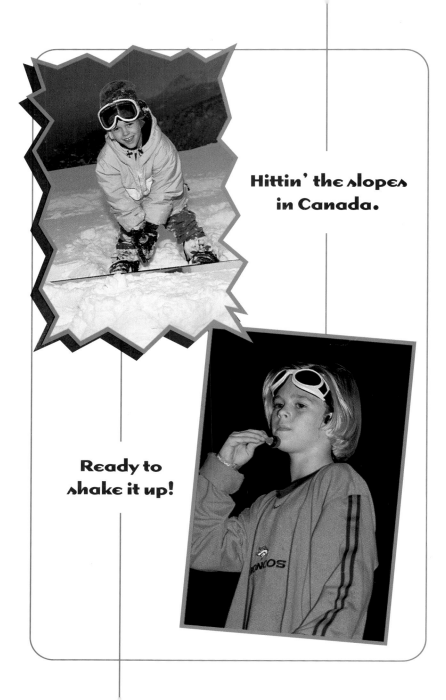

Hittin' the slopes
in Canada.

Ready to
shake it up!

With twin sister Angel.

Heating up the stage in Los Angeles.

Ain't he cute?

**When it comes to his music,
Aaron is serious!**

Cooling off at the beach.

Aaron has always looked up to big bro Nick.

**Aaron loves to hang
with the Backstreet Boys!**

that he has very little trouble memorizing songs and learning new ones.

So that's the scoop on Aaron the Sagittarian! He's so much like his sign, it almost makes you feel like you should seriously start checking out *your* astrological charts and daily horoscopes!

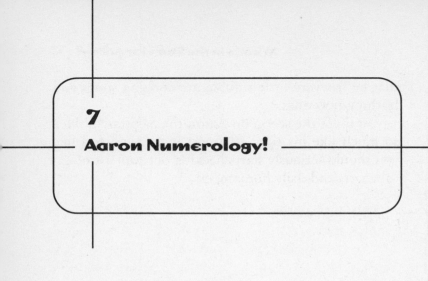

7
Aaron Numerology!

What's Aaron's Number?

Numerology has been around for ages. According to this intriguing numerical science, the numbers, which are called "expression numbers" and "destiny numbers," represent letters. These numbers then translate into one of nine specific categories that describe your personality traits and talents. In essence, it allows you to get the inside scoop on the people you love most, like...Aaron!

Figuring out Aaron's number is a cinch! Just find the numeric value for each letter of his full birth name, Aaron Charles Carter. For example, A is 1, R is 9, etc....(See chart on page 48.) Add up the numbers and keep adding them till you end up with a one-digit number. Then find the number corresponding to the list below and see if the characteristics fit! Aaron's number works out to be a 9.

When it comes to Aaron Carter, he just seems to fit every prediction expert numerologists have made. Here's the deal—people falling under the number 9 category, are said to be creative, and that is *soooo* Aaron! First off, just look at his slick style. He's always wearing bright, colorful, funky clothes. Secondly, he's a singer. For anyone to be able to sing and dance the way he does, he'd have to be creative and artistic.

Nines are compassionate and sympathetic to others. They love to offer their help to those in need. Aaron once said if he had only a few wishes, one would be to make all of the sick people in the world feel better. His participation in the Bravo All-Stars project shows how he cares for children in need.

Nines are people who are always looking out for others and trying to change the world. And 9's have terrific imaginations! They can create wonderful drawings and design new things.

It is said that when 9's are not given the right amount of respect or attention, they can act aloof. Since Aaron is the youngest, he may be used to getting lots of attention. Fans are sure to agree that Aaron seems to fit into his category rather nicely.

Now that you're a little more familiar with numerology, why not find out what your number is? Just follow the chart on the next page, and remember that numerology is just for fun!

1	2	3	4	5	6	7	8	9
A	B	C	D	E	F	G	H	I
J	K	L	M	N	O	P	Q	R
S	T	U	V	W	X	Y	Z	

1—Strong-willed, creative, aggressive, confident, possessing leadership qualities yet sometimes very candid are ways to define this number. These people know how to get things done. The down side to number 1's is that they tend to be self-centered and egotistical and can be hard to live with. Fear of loneliness and being left out of a group can be attributed to those in this category.

2—Peacemaker, cooperative, considerate of others, and friendly are qualities associated with this number. Number 2's are very organized and detail-oriented people who rarely overlook anything of importance. They sometimes don't get the credit they deserve for things, but since they're not self-centered, this doesn't affect them much. On the dark side, those in this category can be shy and easily hurt.

3—Number 3's are usually really good communicators, very diplomatic, slick, and very hip. They are usually excellent singers, actors, and entertainers. It's surprising that Aaron isn't in this category. These folks are positive thinkers, charming, and easygoing types. In fact, they are so easygoing that they tend to spread themselves too thin and are also a little superficial. Style is very important to people who fall under this category—3's love looking good!

4—People falling in this category usually are very responsible, reliable, loyal, and logical. These are the students who work the hardest on their science project or put in extra hours at their weekend job at the Gap. They can sometimes be a little too hard on themselves and are sometimes the envy of others who feel they can't compete with the 4's' ability to impress others.

5—Number 5's are multi-talented, adventurous, energetic, and total charmers who can juggle several things all at one time. They are freethinkers who are very quick and on the ball. Usually, it's a 5 who will finish that math quiz first—especially since they have a great knack for analyzing things. Fives are also very popular. They're the ones who are invited to every party, the people everyone wants to know. Their negative quality is impatience. These people often cannot do certain things for long periods of time without getting restless.

6—Those who fall under this category are conservative, fair, honest, hard workers who usually like a quiet lifestyle. These people are very loving and respectful of others. They have a certain understanding that makes them very generous and giving. These are the people whom you want as boyfriends or girlfriends! The only negative side to 6's is that they expect too much from themselves. They're also worriers.

7—These people are very logical, spiritual, and have a deep need to find out the truth. They are very good at judging and observing their surroundings. They make good teachers and psychics—they can often sense what's about to happen. These are the friends who offer you help with homework or are great at showing you how to figure something out. Their best subjects in school would most likely be science or religious studies. The thing about 7's is that even their closest friends don't know them as well as they think—these people tend to mask a lot of their feelings or keep dark secrets. Sevens often lack expression and can be overly critical and tend to trust no one.

8—Eights are known for setting important career goals and are full of ambition! These people can sometimes be headstrong and stubborn, but in a good way! They know what they want from life. You 8's seriously love to shop! The idea of a new toy or a new item of clothing simply makes your day! And we're not talking everyday inexpensive gear...no, no, no!

You like stylish brand names that will turn heads; you tend to "dress to impress." You're a darling person—just try to work on worrying less about material things and concentrate on things that have a deeper meaning.

9—For a description of this category, just check back to page 47, since Aaron's name works out to be a 9!

8

Are You the Perfect Girl for Aaron?

Like his older brother, Aaron has a huge girl following. He doesn't think that he's ever really been in love. When *Big!* asked him if he'd ever had a girlfriend, Aaron responded, "No way. I'm far too young!" He did admit to having had little crushes in the past, though: "I don't really have a crush on anyone at the moment. I kind of had a crush on the older girl who was in my video. She was really sweet to me."

"Lots of my friends at school have girlfriends, but I haven't," Aaron told journalist Rav Singh. "I'd rather zoom around on the motorcycle Nick gave me." Aaron's mom would agree that her son is still a little too young for girls. He's also way busy with his career. Being a pop star means having a hectic schedule. Aaron is hardly ever home! He's constantly visiting other states and countries to record, promote, and perform.

Aaron has stated that he believes fifteen is the proper age to begin dating. Until then, he'd rather just have girls as friends. When the time is right to find that special girl, however, he does have some requirements. He admits that he's been partial to girls with curly brown hair, but he thinks that personality is more important. "She doesn't have to look like anything in particular, except that she will have to...have a nice personality," Aaron revealed to *SuperTeen*.

Having fun is a priority for Aaron. Most likely, he wouldn't want to date a pouting, sour girl. She should probably be a little wacky and have a wild side to her. Aaron's a bundle of energy, so she'd need to be able to keep up with him. But when *TV Hits* asked him if he preferred crazy to serious girls, Aaron said: "It doesn't matter to me, just so long as she's nice."

He'd probably love it, though, if his future girl thought boating and fishing were fun, since it'd probably make a cool date for the two of them. Aaron might like to take his date to an amusement park, since he loves rides. He's never actually been on a date, but he did dance with German pop star Blümchen once at the Viva Comet Awards show party. Blümchen, which means "little flower" in German, is famous all over Germany and Europe. Her real name is Jasmin Wagner, and she's about two years younger than Nick. She's very pretty and loves cheerleading, horses, and listening to music. She even worked with Aaron and the Bravo All-Stars on the song "Let the Music Heal Your Soul." They also participated in the video together. But they're just friends in the biz—not to mention she's a lot older!

As for the distant future, Aaron told *SuperTeen* reporters that he does plan on getting married someday. Right now he's very self-sufficient for a preteen. Cooking isn't something he's totally into, but he never hesitates to throw some popcorn into the microwave or heat a can of soup. Aaron, like Nick, has told reporters that he can also cook eggs, but pizza is his favorite food. No doubt he'd think that hitting the local pizza place would also make a fun date!

So how do you know whether or not you and Aaron would be a match made in heaven? For fun, why not check out what the stars have to say about you and your favorite singing and dancing cutie? Just find your zodiac sign and read on to see what type of couple you might make. Remember, horoscopes are entertaining, but they're just for fun!

Sagittarius/Aries: Both of these signs love to stay up late and are afraid of missing something. You guys would never think of leaving a party early! Both signs are also somewhat nosy, and friends often tell them to "butt out!" Be careful, though: you guys are both accident-prone. This is so true of Aaron—he's got the scars to prove it! Sag and Aries are also into helping people, so it's possible you might both be involved in raising money for sick children.

Perfect Date: A midnight movie, a wild party, or a charity event.

Sagittarius/Taurus: Tranquil Taurus and spunky Sagittarius always seem to bring out the best in each other, so you and Aaron would make a great team! Sagittarius is very generous, but as a Taurus, you must remember not to take advantage of money or affections. Taurus is known to be moody and sometimes gloomy. The thing is, Sagittarius is usually very upbeat and may not have patience for Taurus's crankiness. Taurus has a thing for cash, but unlike the impulsive-spending Sag, the Taurus is more apt to save cash for a rainy day.

Perfect Date: Something where you put your heads together and make money—have a garage sale or collect cans for recycling!

Sagittarius/Gemini: These two signs generally get along well together. If Aaron was your boyfriend, he might smother you a little bit—since he's a fire sign and Gemini is air! Gemini does enjoy the warmth and inspiration Sag gives, though. You're both very daring and supportive of each other. Your relationship will last a long time. Just beware of playing head games with the super-sensitive Sag!

Perfect Date: Both signs are artistic, so why not get some clay and make something cool together or visit a local museum?!

Sagittarius/Cancer: Cancers are very sensitive types. As a Sagittarian, Aaron needs to feel accepted and loved. In time, you two will become best buds,

and as soon as he knows you share a mutual crush—
he'll be cool. Sags are known for saying whatever's on
their minds, but they must be careful around Cancers!
Cancer's symbol is the crab, and they can really pinch
back! Like Taurus, Cancer has a tendency to be rather
moody, so if Aaron was your man, he'd have to tiptoe
around you sometimes. It's a fact that Sag likes to play
practical jokes (Aaron's admitted this in several interviews) on unsuspecting Cancer. You guys would make
a fun couple—very spirited!

Perfect Date: Something cultural, such as a school
play, would be fun.

Sagittarius/Leo: Playful Sagittarians and fun-lov-
ing Leos make for an adventurous, jolly duo. You
both view life as one big adventure. Since you both
love seeing new places and trying new things, you'd
make perfect travel companions. As long as you guys
are doing something fun and keeping busy, you'll
make a fabulous team. You both are willing to cooper-
ate, which is always a positive thing in a friendship.

Perfect Date: Going on a boat ride or something
really exciting—a ride on a wild roller coaster would
work perfectly!

Sagittarius/Virgo: Sensitive Virgo can be easily
hurt by blunt Sag ways. A Sagittarian has to think
before speaking to super-sensitive Virgo. You are both
very good communicators and have a special understanding of each other, so expect high phone bills if

you and Aaron were to become an item! Sagittarius will have to help loosen Virgo up, and Virgo will have to teach Sag to relax and not be so hyper. Aaron's not shy and neither are you, so it's not hard to imagine you guys putting on silly skits or holding hands in public.

Perfect Date: A concert, since you both love music!

Sagittarius/Libra: Okay, you're totally calm, cool, and collected—but Aaron, being a Sag, has the tendency to be rather restless. Both signs sort of mellow each other out and end up getting along really well. You may find yourselves chatting the night away online or on the phone.

Perfect Date: A teen coffeehouse or the mall is a great place for you two to become better acquainted.

Sagittarius/Scorpio: Sagittarians such as Aaron are always friendly and open, and know how to get their point across. Scorpio, on the other hand, is not always direct and open. Sagittarius doesn't really hide anything, but you Scorpios tend to be secretive. You are also very sensitive, so blunt Sagittarians had better think before they speak! You and Aaron will make a fun couple, but arguments might occur often. Sag likes freedom and Scorpio has a sense of obligation, so you'll have to compromise on certain topics.

Perfect Date: Something competitive, as both signs love a good game! Get a bunch of friends together and play a game of soccer or baseball.

Sagittarius/Sagittarius: What a couple! You both love taking care of each other, and at the same time you're both independent. Since Sag likes to have the upper hand, there may be some arguments, but if you work together to come to a harmonious conclusion, fun times will come your way. You both love a good game of sports or something else that will test your skills.

Perfect Date: A day at the local arcade or at home with Nintendo or PlayStation would be perfect—this way you can challenge each other to video games!

Sagittarius/Capricorn: Capricorns like to seek the truth. They like to be active and involved in social events like parties and get-togethers. As a Capricorn, you may be a little controlling. This won't work well for you and Aaron. Because he's a free-spirited Sag, you'll have to chill out and let him be independent. Sag also likes to be boss, so there may be a power struggle between you two. For example, when it's time to select the movie or where you want to get ice cream, a little tiff might break out. Be careful! Hear each other out and you'll make a great team. Compromise is important.

Perfect Date: Shopping at the mall. Both signs love treating themselves!

Sagittarius/Aquarius: Aquarians are totally independent people who love to socialize and experience new things. Since Aaron likes traveling (he's said it's one of the best things about being a famous singer), the two of you would make excellent partners. Hiking and camping, especially with family and friends, is something you both surely would enjoy.

Perfect Date: Mountain climbing or a day trip to a nearby city, where you'd get a chance to explore!

Sagittarius/Pisces: This is a challenging, yet very interesting, combo. You as a Pisces need to chill when it comes to arguments, like which movie to see. You are both very spiritual people and may enjoy attending houses of worship together. Sagittarians are more into seeking the truth and being open and honest, while Pisces sometimes like to stretch the truth to get around their real feelings. You both will need to work on ways to communicate with each other.

Perfect Date: Studying together, but in a place where you won't disturb anyone—you may end up getting into heated debates about religion or history.

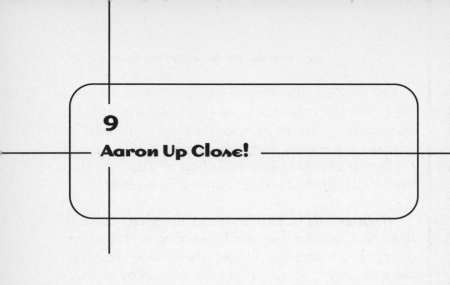

9
Aaron Up Close!

Full Name: Aaron Charles Carter.

Nicknames: "Big A" (Producer and songwriter Gary Carolla gave him that one), "AC" (Backstreet Boys gave Aaron the name when he opened for them in Berlin), "Airboy," and his dad sometimes calls him "Airhead."

Birth Date: December 7, 1987.

Astrological Sign: Sagittarius.

Parents: Jane and Robert (Bob).

Siblings: Ginger (his oldest sister from his dad's first marriage); Nick, Bobbi Jean (also known as B. J.); Leslie Barbara; twin sister, Angel Charissma (two minutes older).

Birthplace: Tampa General Hospital in Tampa, Florida.

Currently Lives: Ruskin, Florida. (A rumor says he may move to California in the near future!)

Height: Approximately 4' 7"—and growing!

Weight: Approximately 70 lbs.

Shoe Size: 5.

Eye Color: Brown.

Hair Color: Blond.

Grade: Fifth.

Schools Attended: Frank D. Miles Elementary School and Ruskin School (Elementary) until about the third grade.

Pets: A guard dog, Simba, two miniature schnauzers named Salty and Pepper, and a seven-foot-long iguana named Babyface. He also has a white-with-black-masked-face Hemingway cat named Bandit, and a tiger kitten named Lucky.

Hobbies: Fishing, boating, snorkeling, swimming, rollerblading, riding Jet Skis, surfing, riding his four-wheeler and mini motorcycle, skateboarding, basketball, video games.

Instruments Played: Saxophone, guitar, and drums.

Worst Habit: Occasionally exaggerating or making up tall tales!

Personality Traits: Fun, hyper, playful, loving, comical, affectionate, and kind.

These Are a Few of His Favorite Things!

Colors: Blue and green.

Movies: *Face/Off, Dragonheart,* any action film!

TV Shows: *The Wonder Years, Johnny Bravo, South Park,* and most cartoons.

***South Park* Characters:** Kenny and Cartman.

Foods: Pizza, sushi, and McDonald's. (Don't feed Aaron corn, he hates it!)

Beverage: Sprite and Coca-Cola—Aaron says it gives him energy before a show!

Candy: Twix chocolate bars and M&M's with peanuts.

Cereal: Count Chocula.

Ice Cream Flavor: Chocolate.

Clothes: Funky urban styles from Tommy Hilfiger, Tomster USA, Adidas, Fila, and Nike.

Dream Car: A Lamborghini.

Hobbies: Collecting Tamagotchis (he has thirty!) and Beanie Babies.

Beanie Babies: Pinchers (the lobster), Radar (the bat), and the Sting (the manta ray).

Video Games: James Bond and Mario

Actress: Tiffani-Amber Thiessen of *90210* fame.

Actor: Sylvester Stallone and Arnold Schwarzenegger.

Book: *Goosebumps* series.

Part of His Body: Hair

Type of Music: Hip-hop, funky dance music.

Groups: BSB, Metallica, Tom Petty and the Heartbreakers, Lynyrd Skynyrd, 'N Sync, Babyface, Dr. Dre, and Mariah Carey.

BSB Song: "As Long as You Love Me."

Songs on His CD: "I'm Gonna Miss You Forever" and "Shake It."

Holidays: Christmas and his birthday, because they're times to be with family, as well as to give and receive gifts!

Sports Teams: Tampa Bay Buccaneers, Florida Marlins, and Oakland A's.

Perfect Day: Munching on candy and spending the day fishing with his family on the boat.

10
100 Fun Facts!

1. Aaron has several scars on his face, including one on the bridge of his nose (the result of a run-in with the hatch on the family boat—he passed out cold!).

2. Aaron has skateboarded with Diana Ross's sons. Ms. Ross is very friendly with the Carters and the Backstreet Boys.

3. Aaron once beat out his own brother in a Swedish popularity poll for best male musician! A reader's survey featured in *Starz* magazine stated that Aaron received 50 percent of the votes, with big brother Nick lagging way behind him with only 12 percent!

4. He's a total collector! Besides collecting Beanies and Tamagotchis, Aaron loves Ninja Turtles. He told a *SuperTeen* reporter he had about five hundred!

5. The littlest Carter appears to be a bit accident-prone. In addition to scarring his nose, he nearly lost

his right foot when he got too close to a boat pro-
peller. He also had a terrible experience
that he'll never forget. When he was just a toddler,
Aaron almost drowned in a swimming pool, but
luckily his dad did CPR and helped jump-start his
breathing. Someone had left the gate to the pool
open. His mom was at work, and Nick and B. J. were
playing in the pool.

6. When touring, Aaron loves to play Nintendo in his
hotel room.

7. Aaron has family in Texas and Kansas. When he or
the Backstreet Boys play a venue in a particular city,
area friends and family always try to come out and
show their support!

8. One time, a doctor had to give him stitches in his
foot. Aaron must have totally hated them, because he
actually removed them himself! *Ouch!*

9. Aaron is afraid of spiders!

10. Aaron has a scar on his lip from having been bit-
ten by a dog.

11. Nick bought Aaron his most prized possession, a
saxophone, which he sometimes takes on the road
with him.

12. Aaron loves the Spice Girls. If he had to be a Spice

Girl, he'd be Baby Spice, because like Emma, he's the youngest!

13. One of his most embarrassing moments occurred in a swimming pool! In an interview with *Top of the Pops* magazine, Aaron said, "I was in an outdoor swimming pool trying to learn this new dive where I bounce off the slide on my butt, only it went wrong and Nick started laughing at me. When I climbed out of the pool...I pretended there was nothing wrong... He laughed even more."

14. Speaking of embarrassing moments...Aaron confessed this incident to *Big!*: "I went out on my motorbike and it went out of control and I skidded over our dog...my sister Angel saw it happen and ran back into the house to tell everyone. Luckily, our dog Simba was okay, but my mom was screaming at me!"

15. Aaron snores! Aaron told *Top of the Pops*, "Nick doesn't snore, but I do, all the time! But not loud enough to wake him up, like Angel does..."

16. When he was younger, he was sometimes scared to sleep alone, especially if he had just seen a scary movie or awakened from a nightmare!

17. Aaron and Angel celebrated their tenth birthday with an awesome-looking cake and a special guest, Mickey Mouse, at Disney World!

18. Nick bought him a motorcycle. "Actually Nick bought me my favorite thing in the whole world, my motorcycle. It's…really, really cool. My dad's built me, like, a mile-long ramp and I jump it and everything," Aaron told *TV Hits* magazine.

19. Aaron loves sleeping on planes. Brother Nick hates flying.

20. He once had an iguana named Mariah Carey, but according to Aaron, his other iguana fatally attacked her out of jealousy.

21. Aaron's sister also used to have a Scottish terrier named Boo Boo, who sadly drowned in 1996.

22. It's like the *Odd Couple*'s Felix and Oscar when it comes to the Carter bros! The guys share a room, and Aaron once confessed to a reporter for *TV Hits* magazine, "I'm very neat, but Nick's really messy. We don't even keep half a room each! Nick's stuff is all over the place, and I end up picking it all up for him!"

23. In an interview with *Big!*, Aaron said that the worst part about being a celebrity was not being able to do "normal things." For example, "Not being able to walk down the street to McDonald's without people recognizing and chasing me."

24. Aaron once started his own Web site and named

MTV's site as one of his favorite sites on the Web!

25. Angel starred alongside him in the "Shake It" video, and Nick also had a cameo in one of Aaron's videos!

26. Since Aaron can't attend regular classes while he's on the road, he needed to hire a tutor. Did you know Nick's former tutor, Mary Cofaud, is also Aaron's tutor and a friend of the family?

27. His favorite school subjects are music and math.

28. Aaron keeps a journal when he's touring. His tutor suggested it.

29. If he could meet anyone in the world, it'd be Michael Jackson.

30. Many times his older sisters baby-sit for him when their parents aren't home.

31. Aaron gets tons of fan mail. He told *SuperTeen,* "I get over eight hundred pieces of mail a day."

32. Did you know he's shy about becoming a famous singer? He didn't want to tell his friends and school-mates! Apparently, word got out when someone spotted his picture in a magazine! *Oops!*

33. Aaron likes to use Rembrandt toothpaste.

34. He sort of believes in UFOs and aliens.

35. He likes to call the Backstreet Boys "B-HANK"! B as in Brian, H as in Howie, A is for A. J., N stands for Nick, and K is for Kevin!

36. He once chipped a tooth. "I have a cap on my front tooth. I did a backflip off some monkey bars and chipped it," Aaron told a *Smash Hits* reporter.

37. Aaron often has a 10:00 P.M. bedtime.

38. There are many posters of the Spice Girls on his side of the bedroom.

39. Nick's given him many presents that he must really treasure. Last May, he told a reporter for *Barbie* magazine about a necklace Nick bought for him. "I've worn it night and day…it always reminds me of Nick, even if he's not with me."

40. Fans often give him special presents, including a teddy bear he calls "Chocolate Carter." He told *Smash Hits:* "I got him from a fan in Spain. I get lots of stuff, but he caught my eye. He goes everywhere with me. I have a GameBoy too, but CC's better. He can speak Spanish, Japanese, and German. He can speak all languages!"

41. He can't date until he's fifteen.

42. Aaron doesn't really have a specific type of girl in mind for his future. "I like the type of girl who is very fun. It doesn't really matter what they look like," stated Aaron in an interview in *SuperTeen* magazine.

43. Aaron likes to play soccer, especially with his sister Angel.

44. He's met Hanson, but didn't really spend much time with them. In several teen magazines, Aaron described meeting them as like "meeting friends."

45. When he's touring, he tries to sleep late in order to be in high-energy form for his concerts!

46. His sister B. J. portrayed the love interest in a video for the young German singer Gil.

47. Aaron's mom played basketball in high school. During an interview with a Canadian television reporter, Aaron said, "She was a good basketball player! She could do front handsprings!"

48. If he could play a part in a movie, Aaron once admitted he'd love to play the character Dennis the Menace.

49. When Nick is home, he sometimes takes Aaron for rides in his Corvette.

50. Aaron's dream car may be a Lamborghini, but he'd also settle for a Porsche or a BMW.

51. Aaron once bought his sister Leslie a gold necklace. In an interview with *Top of the Pops*, Aaron said, "I once bought my sister Leslie a real nice gold necklace. It was really expensive…It has a star at the end filled with millions of real diamonds…"

52. His dad bought him a bike as a present.

53. He has a friend named Michael who lives across the water. How does he get there? "I either ride my bike around or sail over in the boat," Aaron told a reporter.

54. Aaron and his sister often play football. "We play when we have the chance, but it's usually Angel who wins," he declared during an interview with a British mag.

55. Aaron may be from a big family, but his dad, Robert, was an only child.

56. Aaron's dad has a cool tattoo of the Warner Brothers character Taz!

57. His big brother Nick's middle name is Gene. It's after their father, Robert Gene.

58. Aaron loves indulging in sneakers! He has many

pairs, including Nikes and Skechers.

59. If he had to select a favorite month out of the year, it would probably be December! During that month, Aaron celebrates not only his birthday, but his favorite holiday, too—Christmas!

60. Aaron says he'd love to do a TV series.

61. He's right-handed.

62. He is not really a worrier and rarely gets nervous.

63. Sometimes being young isn't so fun. When Aaron tours with other groups, they like to attend late-night parties after gigs. Since he's only eleven, he usually has to hit the sack or play video games in his room. This was also the case for Nick! He was the youngest Backstreet Boy, and while the others could go to the eighteen-and-over dance clubs, Nick would usually have to pass.

64. Sometimes when he's traveling, he writes songs.

65. If you ever meet Aaron, he would appreciate it if you were calm and friendly. Some fans pull his hair and grab at him. This must make him very uncomfortable.

66. His mom, Jane, picks out most of his clothes, especially for the videos. Aaron has to agree with the items she picks, but she knows his style. They're almost always on the same wavelength when it comes to style.

67. His mom's picture has been in so many magazines, she sometimes has to wear her hair differently or put on sunglasses so Aaron's fans won't swarm around her.

68. Nick and Aaron's mom helps manage his career and makes sure everything runs smoothly.

69. Sometimes his sisters will come to the studio when he's recording.

70. He likes to put his siblings in his videos. Nick had a cameo in one video, and Angel had a big part in "Shake It."

71. Biscuit used to be Aaron's bodyguard (he was also the New Kids on the Block's and 'N Sync's bodyguard) and was his tour manager in 1998!

72. Both Aaron and Angel have the exact same initials, A.C.C.!

73. His favorite teacher was named Miss Matthews.

74. Aaron likes to give his family gifts. He once made his mom a shirt in school for Mother's Day. The shirt described why mothers are special, and Jane says she'll treasure it forever.

75. Rumor has it Aaron was named after his grandfather, Aaron Charles Carter, and that he likes it when people call him "Chuckie," since that was his grandpa's nickname also.

76. He once lost his suitcase during a flight from Madrid. When they discovered this, Aaron quickly went on a shopping spree in London and bought some new jeans and shirts!

77. Aaron came in second at a talent show held at the Rock School.

78. Aaron's bodyguard during his North American tour was a close friend of Nick's named Mike.

79. His mom was around twenty-seven years old when he was born.

80. Aaron's dog saved him once. He rolled into the pool, and Simba jumped in and brought him to safety.

81. Aaron has an Uncle Steve.

82. Nick has thought about going into the military.

83. Nick and Aaron often take their dogs with them on family camping trips.

84. When a *SuperTeen* reporter visited Aaron's home, he found Aaron eating a McDonald's Arch Deluxe.

85. At this same interview, Aaron showed the reporter and photographer what was inside his family's fridge, which by the way, is the type that fills your glass with ice and cold water! Among shelves of leftovers was a bottle of Sunny D! *Yum!*

86. Aaron has about ten awards for making music.

87. His album has gone platinum in Canada.

88. Aaron has a little fountain/wishing well and a trampoline in his yard !

89. His sister Leslie helped him learn to ride his motorcycle.

90. Aaron has admitted that he likes to show off in front of his siblings and their friends by doing stunts.

91. When he rides Jet Skis with his dad, he almost always falls off.

92. He once saw a shark and a dolphin. His mom taught him that dolphins like to chase sharks away.

When they take the boat to Key West, they sometimes see dolphins.

93. He has a videotape about wild animals and watches it all the time.

94. His sister Leslie has more of a folk voice and sometimes gets shy singing in front of a small group or people she knows.

95. He loves Tommy Hilfiger and even wears Hilfiger socks! In an interview with *SuperTeen*, Aaron said he wouldn't mind being sponsored by the designer.

96. Aaron, like most boys, loves making funny noises and silly faces to make people laugh.

97. Of all the Backstreet Boys, he's closest to Brian and thinks Kevin is the most serious, since he's the oldest.

98. He's a big fan of *South Park* and loves to imitate the characters, just like Backstreet Boys A. J. and Nick.

99. Aaron likes to watch CNN when he travels.

100. Nick sings background vocals on Aaron's song "Please Don't Go Girl." Aaron's album took only ten weeks to make!

11
Aaron Online!

There are dozens of fabulously informative Aaron Carter Web sites. However, you will notice that many of these sites are dedicated to Aaron *and* Nick, which is very cool since you get the scoop on *two* adorable babes at the same time.

If you have a Web site that you think is just as hot as the ones about to be mentioned, then be sure to contact the owners of the following sites and request that they add your page as a link. Most fans that own sites are very helpful and are willing to help out, just as long as you link yours to theirs. After all, it is only fair!

One of the best things about the fan sites is that they provide a place for Aaron and Nick fans to unite and share info. You'll find tons of new pals through Web sites, since many of them offer Aaron chat rooms where you can talk about Aaron or anything related to Nick or the Backstreet Boys. There are often message boards where you can leave messages, questions, or info for other fans to see and respond to. Many sites have a forum for pen pals or e-mail pals to exchange info and hook up. Keep in mind that not everyone on the Web is honest, so be sure never to reveal personal info in public areas such as message boards and chat rooms. Some sites offer an area where fans can trade, sell, or buy Aaron posters, pictures, and other cool things. But beware of scammers when making deals over the Internet. Be sure your parents have okayed the deal and that you can trust the trader. Remember, you should never send cash through the mail.

Whenever you're surfing the Web for your favorite singer, group, or actor, it's always wise to access the official site first. The official site is the site that's been approved by the performer and his management. The information included there is the most accurate, but it may not be the most up-to-date. Be advised that some of these fan pages may no longer still be in existence by the time you read this. Often, Web masters decide that because of schoolwork or other interests, they no longer have the time to run their site.

Below are the most sizzling Aaron Carter Web sites that will have you pointing and clicking your way into Aaron heaven in minutes!

Aaron's Official Web Site

www.aaroncarter.com

As soon as you arrive at Aaron's Official Web Site, several things will stand out. First, get a load of the dancing animated Aaron! How precious is that? Another thing is that the purples, yellows, and other funky colors really catch your eye. This site includes all the basic info on Aaron. His bio and other press info can be found here, as well as a link to Edel Records, his record label.

Aaron's Own Personal Web Site
members.wbs.net/homepages/a/a/i/aairboy.html

With luck, by the time you're reading this, Aaron's personal site will still be posted. It is a very basic site. You'll notice that it has an "Under Construction" sign attached to it, and that there is a very limited amount of information listed within the page. However, you'll want to take a look at it simply because it was created by Aaron himself! Aaron starts off by saying, "Hello! My name is Aaron Carter! I am Nick Carter's youngest brother!..." He also includes his age, an address to write to him, and links to his favorite sites, which include his mom's site, big sister B. J.'s site, MTV, and others. This site is cool because it makes you feel as if you really know him when you click on the links he chose himself!

Carter World
www.come.to/carterworld

This is, by far, truly the most amazing Aaron and Nick fan site you will find on the Web. The site was created in October 1997 and is maintained by two fif-teen-year-old Canadian fans named Henna and Elspeth. Together, the girls make a great team, with Henna doing most of the writing and Elspeth doing the scanning of photos!

The newsroom is a place where fans from all over the world—from India to Italy—post the latest Aaron, Nick, and Backstreet Boys news. There is a list of a hundred facts about Nick and Aaron as well as a chat room, an area where you can purchase Aaron and Nick-related items, and so much more. CarterWorld features artwork sent in by fans and sometimes runs contests and polls.

Before exiting this amazing Web site, be sure to sign up for their e-mail newsletter. It's free and will keep you updated on the latest info, in case you don't have a chance to constantly check the site. Nick him-self may be a subscriber to her newsletter—but Henna can't say for sure. She can only base it on an e-mail address that looks awfully fishy! Henna and Elspeth keep you totally in tune to what's going on with your favorite singers, so you have to make sure you stop by their site as soon as possible.

The Carter Cuties
www.angelfire.com/nc/ngaccarter/index.html

This site was started in March 1998 and is run by two fans, one from Malaysia and the other from the U.S.A. There are plenty of cool things to check out once you reach this site. You're welcomed to the Carter Cuties site with adorable pictures of Aaron and Nick. You need to click onto them in order to enter the site. Once you're inside, find out info on Nick *or* Aaron. You'll love the section filled with answers to tons of questions and rumors related to Nick, Aaron, the Carters, and the Backstreet Boys! Does your love for Aaron and/or Nick inspire you to get creative and write a poem or story? No problem, because the Carter Cuties Web site encourages you to submit and display personal poems or stories you've written about either Carter brother! Click on different spots for up-to-date news, take a poll, check out the latest rumors, post a message on their message boards, and, of course, download tons of sweet pictures of Nick and Aaron. All in all, an excellent site!

Nick & Aaron Carter Planet
www.geocities.com/Broadway/Alley/2182/index.html

Upon arriving at this sizzling site, you're treated to a MIDI version of "Quit Playin' Games (with My Heart)," which lets you know to expect only good things from Nick & Aaron Carter Planet! This site has incredible photos not only of both brothers but also of their parents and sisters. Wanna send a Nick or Aaron Internet card to a friend? No problem, this site—like many others—has that feature. Only this one gives you the option of sending music along with it! This way, as your bud is downloading pictures of

Aaron, he or she can listen to his songs "Shake It" or "Swing It Out"! Very cool, indeed!

Cyrus & Kristin's Aaron Carter
www.geocities.com/SunsetStrip/Backstage/3836/aaron.htm

Like the other Aaron sites, you will find darling photos of him, along with biographical information, lyrics to his songs, Aaron Carter Real Audio, and lots more!

The Carter Brothers
www.geocities.com/Hollywood/Studio/9862

The Carter Brothers site is run by a seventeen-year-old girl from Sydney, Australia, named Belinda. In addition to loving Aaron, she's also way into the Backstreet Boys and Hanson. According to Belinda, "Aaron is really cute and so talented for his age!"

When you reach Belinda's site, you are asked to click on the brother you want information about. Her site features a pen pal section, tons of articles on Aaron and Nick, and a place to swap info. Be sure to send a friend an electronic postcard with a cute picture of Nick or Aaron! There is also a Web ring and links to other cool sites.

Rosa's Aaron Carter Page
members.wbs.net/homepages/a/a/r/aaroncarterpage.html

Be sure to check out Rosa's page! It's crammed with baby pix of Aaron, tons of interviews from various international magazines, and cool interviews in Real Audio that you can download and listen to. There's even a place where you can download Nick and Aaron wallpaper for either your computer or your Web site! Before you exit, don't forget to take Rosa's Aaron quiz. Be prepared—it's not exactly a piece of cake!

Other Cool Aaron Sites!

www.geocities.com/SunsetStrip/Venue/8675/index.html
home-2.worldonline.nl/~dkamp/index/nick.html
www.geocities.com/SunsetStrip/Frontrow/9944
www.airboycarter.com
www.angelfire.com/nc/everybodygetwild/index.html
www.angelfire.com/oh/airboyrules/index.html
members.tripod.com/~Shivangi/index-2.html
members.tripod.com/~aaron7
www.expage.com/page/aaroncarterfans
www.geocities.com/SunsetStrip/Amphitheatre/7191/index.html
members.aol.com/Aaron4Me11/acnc.html
www.blueriver.demon.nl/acarter.htm
come.to/aaroncarter
www.angelfire.com/ga/bsb4me/index.html

12
Contact Aaron!

There are many ways for you to let Aaron know just how much you care. He can be reached several different ways. But remember that Aaron receives over eight hundred pieces of fan mail a day, so try to think of clever ways to make your particular letter stand out.

It's always wise to use either vivid colored envelopes or large-sized envelopes. Don't be afraid to get creative. Many celebrities claim that an artistic-looking letter often finds its way into the hands of the person it's meant for instead of a fan mail service. Fan mail services are hired or set up by performers and ensure that each person who sent a note gets something in response. It's the actor's or singer's way of saying thanks. Although many fans hope for something more in response, you have to admit it's better to get a simple typewritten postcard than nothing at all!

So get those pens and art supplies ready and get cracking. Let Aaron know how much you love him or send a self-addressed stamped envelope to his fan club and ask for more info!

Letters to Aaron!

Aaron Carter
P.O. Box 1412
Ruskin, FL 33570 USA

Aaron Carter
c/o Edel America Records, Inc.
1790 Broadway
7th Floor
New York, NY 10019

E-mail Aaron!

Rumor has it that this is Aaron's
personal e-mail address. Good luck!

airboy@usa.net

Official Aaron Fan Club Addresses!

Aaron Carter Fan Club
Postfach 0617
94307 Straubing
Germany
Fax: (+49) 09426/850325

Aaron Carter Fan Info
P.O. Box 8157
London, W2 3GZ
Tel: 0891 600 063

German Fans Can Write to Aaron at:

Aaron Carter
c/o Edel Records GmbH
Wichmannstr. 4
22607 Hamburg
Germany

His Official German Fan Page:

urc1.cc.kuleuven.ac.be/~m9711650

Canadian Aaron Fan Info!

Aaron Carter Information
c/o Attic Records Limited
102 Atlantic Avenue
Toronto, Ontario
M6K 1X9
Canada

German CD Mail Order Info!

Aaron Carter CD Mail Order
Cinema Soundtrack Club
Postfach 520265
22592 Hamburg Germany
Fax: (+49) 040/8905671

13

Bonus Section: All About Nick!

Facts & Stats!

Full Name: Nickolas Gene Carter.

Nicknames: Frack (Backstreet Boy Brian Littrell is known as Frick), Chaos, and Nicky.

Birth Date: January 7, 1980—he's an Aquarius.

Birthplace: Jamestown, New York.

Currently Lives: Ruskin, Florida.

Height: 6'1" (Aaron says he's taller than the Backstreet Boys' oldest member, Kevin Richardson, now!).

Weight: Approximately 160 lbs.

Shoe Size: 11.

Eye Color: Blue.

Hair Color: Blond.

Pets: Two pug dogs named Mikey and Willie and another dog named Houston (he got her when he was doing a show in Houston, Texas!).

Car: A black Corvette, a Camaro, and a forest green truck.

Schools Attended: Frank D. Miles Elementary School and Adams Middle School in Tampa. Nick was taken out of regular school around the age of twelve because of the Backstreet Boys and was tutored until he completed his high school courses.

Hobbies: Fishing, boating, scuba (Nick is a licensed scuba diver), swimming, basketball, video games, etc.

Instruments Played: Vocals, drums, and a little guitar.

Worst Habit: A little addicted to video games and, according to his mom, he's got a major sweet tooth!

Personality Traits: Fun, hyper, comical; can be quiet and shy.

Heritage: Nick told *Bop* magazine that he's Blackfoot Indian and possibly has a bit of Spanish blood in him. This, of course, goes for Aaron, too!

Nicest Thing Ever Given to Him by a Fan: A go-cart for Christmas.

Faves & Raves!

Colors: Forest green

Movies: *Braveheart, Big Trouble in Little China,* and all of the Alien and Ninja Turtles movies, just like Aaron!

TV Shows: *South Park, Mad About You,* and *The X-Files.*

Actor: Bruce Willis and Jeff Goldblum.

Actress: Christina Ricci.

Foods: Pizza, McDonald's, and seafood.

Beverage: Colas. When performing or playing basketball, he likes water and Gatorade!

Candy: Twix chocolate bars and grape-flavored Big League Chew.

Cereal: Frosted Flakes.

Ice Cream Flavor: Chocolate-chip cookie dough.

Pizza: Extra cheese!

Clothes: Funky urban styles from Nike, Tommy Hilfiger, Adidas, Fila, and FUBU.

Hobbies: Collecting Beanie Babies. According to Aaron, Nick has over eighty of 'em!

Video Games: Mortal Kombat, Sony PlayStation's Final Fantasy VII, and many more!

Type of Music: Hip-hop, rock, and alternative.

Groups: Journey, Nirvana, Boyz II Men, Wu-Tang Clan, R. Kelly, and Snoop.

Holidays: "Christmas and Halloween, because there's lots of gifts and candy!" Nick once told *SuperTeen.*

Teams: Tampa Bay Buccaneers and Florida Marlins.

Daydream: Taking his boat down to the Florida Keys with a special girl.

What he can cook: Eggs, Campbell soups, seafood, and barbecue!

Nick's Intimate Secrets!

Nick sleeps in boxers!

Nick wears a silver ring, which he calls a "promise ring," that symbolizes a special friendship with someone.

Nick doesn't think kissing on the first date is wrong. In a KTU radio interview, Nick said he wouldn't be opposed to kissing his date good night.

Nick told fans in a Yahoo! online chat, "In general, what I look for is somebody who can handle the pressures and things that I do. A lot of the reasons we don't have girlfriends is because of all the pressures we undertake. I mean, you have to be attracted to a person, but you can put a not-so-good looking girl next to a gorgeous girl, and if the not-so-good-looking girl has a better personality, then you'll go that way…"

If Nick could perform one miracle, it would be to clean up the ocean!

There have been rumors that Nick will someday get a tattoo. He wants to keep up a family tradition—his dad has one.

Nick received his high school diploma in a hotel room while the Backstreet Boys were on the road!

He's admitted that, unlike Aaron, he's not a huge fan of the Spice Girls.

In an on-line chat, Jane said that Nick has expressed an interest in someday joining the military—his dad was in the military!

Corey Barnes is a New York area–based writer, editor, and reporter who has been covering celebrity events and topics since elementary school. She plans to write more books on popular singers, actors, and other entertainers for young readers to enjoy.